What people are sa

Creating Real Happ

Practicing mindfulness helps you to give up the pursuit of happiness so that you can be happy NOW! This beautiful book shows you how.

Robert Holden, Bestselling Hay House author

Creating Real Happiness A to Z is a wonderful daily guide to help you be in the moment and find peace in the here and now. Stephani's story is especially poignant and her own experience of coming home to herself is an incredible inspiration for anyone questioning if they have what it takes to heal.

Jessica Flanigan, author of *The Loving Diet*

Creating Real Happiness A to Z is packed with wisdom and bite-sized tools for the new and advanced souls on a path of deeper spiritual connection. It is easy to digest, and it offers incredible practical tools that can be used immediately. I highly recommend this wonderful book.

Charmayne Kilcup, author of *Heal Your Heart: How to Awaken Your Soul with Self-Forgiveness*

Creating Real Happiness A to Z

A Mindful Guide to Discovering, Loving,
and Accepting Your True Self

Creating Real Happiness A to Z

A Mindful Guide to Discovering, Loving, and Accepting Your True Self

Stephani Grace

Winchester, UK
Washington, USA

JOHN HUNT PUBLISHING

First published by O-Books, 2022
O-Books is an imprint of John Hunt Publishing Ltd., 3 East St., Alresford,
Hampshire SO24 9EE, UK
office@jhpbooks.com
www.johnhuntpublishing.com
www.o-books.com

For distributor details and how to order please visit the 'Ordering' section on our website.

ISBN: 978 1 78904 951 0
978 1 78904 952 7 (ebook)
Library of Congress Control Number: 2021942987

A CIP catalogue record for this book is available from the British Library.

Design: Matthew Greenfield

UK: Printed and bound by CPI Group (UK) Ltd, Croydon, CR0 4YY
Printed in North America by CPI GPS partners

We operate a distinctive and ethical publishing philosophy in
all areas of our business, from our global network of authors to
production and worldwide distribution.

Contents

For Liv~

Tell me, what is it you plan to do
with your one wild and precious life?
—Mary Oliver

Introduction

I'm happy that you have found your way to this book, and I'm honored to be a part of your spiritual journey. *Creating Real Happiness A to Z* is intended to help you move away from suffering and into your true nature, which is love and acceptance. I've assembled many ideas and practices in an A to Z format to help deepen your relationship with your true self. Each entry will help you learn ways to become more accepting and loving of yourself, ultimately leading you to the life you deserve—one that is free from suffering and full of love.

Most important, please keep in mind that nothing will change without practice. You will notice that there is a lot of repetition in this book—that is intentional. We need to hear the same things over and over to reprogram our thinking. If you are not currently happy then that means something in your life needs to change. Do the recommended exercises, practice one step or letter at a time, and begin to create happiness. I promise that if you practice it will lead you straight to your own heart, to a new level of happy.

My Path to Self-Discovery and Acceptance

My earliest memories are of being alone. I didn't have parents who were capable of loving me. My biological father was an alcoholic and a drug addict, and when I was two years old, he decided to leave my mother. This caused her to flee to Las Vegas and abandon my two older sisters and me, leaving us with my father and his new girlfriend (who would soon become his wife). I only saw my mother briefly two different times during the next five years. My dad and his new wife were deep into their addictions, so I endured a life of neglect and a lack of love.

My two older sisters assumed the majority of my care, but they were not equipped to care for me as they were children themselves. They have told me that they were haunted by my being alone in my crib, wailing for human contact that first year. This set the stage for me in terms of learning that my needs were not important and that I was not worthy of love or care.

When my father's marriage dissolved five years later, I was handed off to my biological mother, whom I didn't know at all. Even though my stepmother hadn't been available or capable of caring for me, she had been the only mother I had known. Having her walk out of my life without a second glance was horribly painful to me, and it was my second abandonment from a mother figure. I was heartbroken by that loss. I would soon come face to face with my mother's mental illness, and the remainder of my childhood would be wrought with confusion, mental abuse, and still more neglect.

Coming from a childhood with adults who didn't know how to love themselves, let alone others, especially their children, left me feeling unlovable and empty. I learned to get attention through achievement and by being *really* good. These elements would come to drive me. I would find myself looking for love in people who could not love me and who were not available. This would begin a cycle for me that would confirm my beliefs about myself: that my needs were not important and that I was unlovable.

Because I spent most of my time alone as a child, I became terrified of being alone. Ironically, in order to learn to love myself, I had to learn to be alone with myself. I did everything I could to avoid being alone. I got married young, and when my marriage failed, I took up drinking like it was my life's purpose. It wasn't until I let go of the drinking and began to truly spend time with myself that I realized that I had been afraid of who I was and that I didn't really know myself at all. This is how my friendship with my true self began. Slowly, one step at a time, I grew to know and love myself. Through my self-discovery, I learned that I was indeed worthy of love and that my needs were the most important. The more I grew to love myself, the more circumstances in my life changed for the better. Knowing my worth opened up opportunities that continued to confirm my worth. I quit attracting selfish, unavailable people and found myself surrounded by loving, available people. The funny thing is, these friends had always been there—I just didn't see them in that way because my mindset was one of lack and of being unlovable. So even if people were willing to love me, I couldn't accept it until I loved myself. Knowing my worth allowed things to come more easily for me. I no longer felt an urgency to control things, because I trusted that all the right steps and opportunities would be presented to me.

I endured a difficult childhood, but I wouldn't change any of it. I believe that as humans we learn best through contrast. I needed to be born into a family that couldn't love me so that I could learn to love myself and in return teach others to love. I have a belief that everything is intended to help us grow into our best, highest selves. In this way of thinking, nothing is trying to harm or punish us. I believe this is the truth because I have learned complete contentment, and I'm not sure I would have understood this love had I not experienced the opposite.

When I am working with people to help them find happiness, I am coming from a place of knowing. I know absolutely that it is possible for anyone to be truly happy, regardless of his or her circumstances or origin. The amazing thing about this is that it is all within our own control. It is all about our conditioning and our beliefs about ourselves and what we think we deserve. When we learn to shift these beliefs, we shift everything.

My entire life I've been drawn to spirituality, and I've been voraciously reading spiritual books nonstop since my late teens. In college I began researching resiliency, because I wanted to understand why some people could rise above adversity while others couldn't. I think spirituality drew me to counseling. For me, it was a natural progression to want to share what I had learned in my own life. I had this deep knowing that it was possible for anyone to create what he or she wanted in his or her life, and I knew that adversity didn't get to determine our life outcome. I had this burning desire to help people understand that adversity wasn't a life sentence. I knew that this was my purpose and that this work was unavoidable for me.

In the work that I do, counseling and spirituality are synonymous. My goal in working with people is to help them learn to love and accept themselves. This is the goal of my work because I believe there is no other way to true happiness. No other way is sustainable; it is merely a fleeting mirage.

My clients are on a journey with me. As I am learning and discovering things in my own life, I weave these teachings into my counseling practice. Anything that I am utilizing in my practice comes from what has worked for me. I have deep empathy for those who suffer, and because I have learned how to create happiness out of struggle, I know that no one should settle for suffering. Therefore, I am tenacious in my patience with others in their search for happiness. I know it's possible to create happiness, and I also know that it's not difficult, although it seems impossible at times. Happiness is always available to us, always within our reach.

I want to help as many people as possible understand this process and to help them learn how to love themselves. I have been in practice for 20 years and have helped hundreds of people find happiness and live a more authentic life. With this book, I hope to reach a wider audience and share the tools that have helped not only me but also my clients. We all deserve to be happy. This is our birthright. Just think how things would shift in our world if we were all coming from a place of absolute self-love.

Conditioning and the Ego

In order for this book to be most helpful to you, it is important for you to have an understanding of both your ego and your true self, and how these two entities operate in your life. Our conditioning from the outside world develops our ego, which is why ego is often referred to as the *conditioned self*. This conditioning comes in the form of our parents, teachers, community, church, peers, and so on. Our ego is based in fear and is developed as a form of protection from the outside world. It thinks it is being helpful by giving us messages it believes we need in order to be safe, loved, and accepted. This conditioning is what causes us to think that we may be anything other than goodness and perfection. We start to question our needs, worth, lovability, and so on. No one is immune to this conditioning and the development of ego—it is part of the human condition. As children we are completely dependent upon the adults in our lives, and if they are unable to meet our needs, we can't help but believe that this means there is something wrong with us, with our needs. This conditioning that we learn growing up remains our truth until we realize that this truth no longer fits for us, and we decide we want a life that feels better and more authentic to our true nature.

We will not be free from ego by rejection, hate, avoidance, or any other negative stance. Integration and freedom from ego will only come from love and acceptance. Ego is a part of our true self, so this is why rejecting this aspect of ourselves won't rid us of the ego. It will only make things worse. Instead we need to understand what this part of us needs in order to heal. Think of your ego as someone you'd like to befriend. In this way you can always approach your ego in a loving and gentle way, from a place of curiosity instead of hate or rejection.

You will know that you are operating out of ego if you don't feel good, such as when you feel depressed or anxious. Your thoughts will be unkind. When you are operating from your true self, your thoughts are never mean or disparaging. When you are operating from ego, life will be difficult and won't flow—

and you'll feel a sense of lack. You may feel like situations are working against you or that things never go in your favor. It will feel difficult to achieve the goals you want for yourself. Basically, if you are not feeling good and you are not at peace then the ego is at work. If you want to feel happier, learn to connect with your true self.

Getting to Know Your True Self

You were born into a physical body as a nonphysical being, which you may know as the soul or the higher self. Throughout this book, I will refer to the nonphysical aspect of ourselves as our "true self." When you first entered your human body, you were aware of your true self. You knew you were divine perfection, that you were nothing but love and goodness. Once the conditioning from the outside world began, you started to lose touch with your true self. You likely began to question your goodness and then you may have felt unlovable or that there was something wrong with you in some way.

At this point, you may not be able to tell the difference between your ego and your true self. Often we have been living completely under the spell of the ego, believing that this is our truth. But it's not. I promise you that. If you are not completely happy and you don't believe yourself to be worthy of everything that you desire in this world then your ego is surely at work. No need to worry; this is to be expected. You've had a lifetime of building up your ego, which has resulted in covering up your true self, making it hard to recognize. Sometimes our true self can have layers and layers of dust on it. As we begin to uncover the dust, it allows the light of our true self to shine through. The most important aspect of getting to know your true self is the desire to do so. If you want to then you will.

The first step in getting to know yourself is to learn to quiet the mind. The mind is not your true self. Only when the mind is quiet can you begin to know what is happening on the inside.

But our minds are quite chaotic, and we can't just make them stop with a snap of a finger. Our minds require training through meditation. Meditation is the best way to practice quieting the mind so we can hear and feel what is happening on the inside. This is how we connect to our true self—in the midst of the quiet. The more we visit our true self in meditation, the easier it is for us to hear it outside of meditation. It also becomes easier to differentiate between the ego and the true self.

It sounds simple and it is, but it's also difficult, so patience and kindness are a must as you begin to know your true self through meditation. The positive news is that it gets easier the more you practice. If you really want to get to know your true self, commit to practicing meditation every single day. If you are sporadic in your practice, it will be like starting fresh each time you do it, and you may find yourself feeling frustrated that things aren't improving and then you're likely to give it up. Make it feel manageable for yourself and something that you know you can sustain. Commit to five minutes a day to start, or if that feels too hard then start with three minutes. The truth is, you have the time available, it's simply a matter of doing it and being consistent. If you want your life to change then you must take the time to practice.

How to Use This Book

Every step is on the path.
—Lao Tzu

All of us tend to become overwhelmed by taking on too much at once. Change can be scary and intimidating, and if we try to implement too many changes at one time, it can make us believe that change is too hard or that we can't do it. Knowing this, I've written this book so that it's approachable. I chose an A to Z format to make it easy for you to take it one step at a time. We can make anything happen by taking it one step at a time. That being said, there is no right way to use this book. Please listen to yourself and honor what you believe will benefit you most and allow you to sustain the practices.

I do recommend reading at least one entry per day and doing the practice. Sometimes a practice will be recommended for a longer period of time, such as a week, so you can focus on completing an exercise before moving onto another if that feels best for you. You can also read it all the way through and come back and do the exercises one at a time or randomly flip to an entry. You don't need to read the entries in order. My hope for you is that you find exercises that resonate with you and become part of your daily practice.

Another important aspect of this book is guidance and inspiration. Wherever you are on your path, I believe that some form of guidance is essential. Without it we all fall prey to having our ego run the show. This book is intended to be a lifelong companion. You can have it on your bedside table to help keep you on your path. Any time you need inspiration or guidance, flip to a page or begin the book again.

"EVERY STEP IS ON THE PATH"

—LAO TZU

Practices and Awarenesses for Staying on
the Path of Love and Acceptance

ACCEPTANCE

Acceptance of "what is" in life is the key to freedom and peace. We often create expectations about how we want things to proceed in our daily lives, and when they don't go this way, we become extremely upset. Understand that things will unfold as they will, and they may not line up with how you wish.

Practice being able to sit with uncomfortable feelings that arise when things don't go your way. Maybe it's a flat tire on your way to work, a relationship ending, or a beloved pet dying. We can practice sitting with the feelings of anger, frustration, sadness, and so on, thereby releasing that energy. Holding on to how it should have been or frustration over being wronged will not change the situation — it will only cause you more suffering.

Our ego makes us believe that feeling these painful feelings will be too painful and intolerable, when in reality this is our key to freedom and to remaining in the present moment. Taking things as they come and feeling the feelings that arise in the moment is acceptance of what is. When we avoid our feelings, we are not actually escaping them, and we will eventually have to deal with these feelings in some way.

It takes practice to not fear pain and to learn that we can tolerate it. The more quickly we feel it, the more quickly we can release it.

Practice: Practice acceptance of *what is* today! Notice your feelings throughout the day, and if you experience wanting things to be different, try being present with this feeling. Bring your gentlest self to this feeling. Practice nurturing yourself from the inside so that your feelings don't get trapped in your body or project onto others. It is nurturing to simply be present with your emotions. You may find that placing one hand on your heart and one hand on your belly is helpful with this process.

AFFIRMATION

Everything is an affirmation. What you choose to wear, eat, think, or buy is an affirmation of your inner self. For example, are you choosing clothing because it makes you feel good and celebrates your personality or are you using it to hide yourself, believing that your body is shameful? If you want to feel good and are practicing loving your body then making a choice that matches this is important. It doesn't feel loving to feel like you have to hide yourself. What kind of message is that sending to yourself? Does the food you eat energize you and make you feel your best? Or do you feel guilty and yucky after eating your choice of food?

Take some time to think about what you want for yourself. How do you want to feel and be reflected in the world? What are your current choices affirming about you? Do your thoughts and actions affirm how you want to feel? If not, what needs to change? How can you begin to make your internal world match what you want for your external world? Usually we need to start with our thoughts. Begin noticing your thinking. If you want to be happy then focus on what is working for you, not on what isn't working. If you want to be successful then you must focus on what you want to create, not how you might fail. If you want to be more healthy, begin thinking of yourself as a healthy person, not berating yourself for choices you've made in the past. Affirm the life you want for yourself!

Practice: Take some time to write about what you want your life to look and feel like. Begin living your life as an affirmation. Choose to spend your time with people who lift you up, wear clothes that make you smile, and eat healthy food that nourishes you and makes you feel good. Begin to notice every action and choice that you make. Is it affirming the life you want? Practice choosing only things that affirm the life that you want for yourself. When you notice that your thoughts and actions aren't a match, simply take some time to shift them to what you do want. Remember, you can always choose again. This could be reframing a negative thought to a more loving thought, choosing not to hang out with certain people again, making a different food choice at your next meal, or getting rid of clothing that makes you feel bad.

APPRECIATION

Fill yourself up by being an appreciator of life. You want to be someone who appreciates life, not someone who depreciates it. Being an appreciator will make you feel good and connect you to your true self, and being a depreciator will not. Take time to notice the beauty that surrounds you and the things that are working in your life, rather than focusing on what you don't like or what isn't working.

Learning to love yourself doesn't mean you have to change or fix yourself first. It means appreciating yourself exactly as you are, even when you want things to be different. Remember, you can always begin again or choose differently at any time.

Practice: Practice being an appreciator today. Take time to notice the things in your life that you appreciate (including yourself).

"Fill yourself up by being an appreciator of life."

AWARENESS

Awareness happens in the present moment. The more you practice being present and in touch with your true self, the more aware you will become. When you are caught in your thoughts (ego), you are unaware of what is happening in the present. When you are not present, you are unaware of how you are actually feeling, how the world is impacting you, and how you are impacting others. When you are dwelling in the past or worrying about the future, you are not in the present and so you are not aware.

We have to practice being aware in order to make the changes we want for ourselves. Awareness is the first step in the process of change. Without awareness it is impossible for us to make changes, which is why practicing awareness is so important. In a sense, it is the most important step in our growth process.

Practice: To strengthen your awareness, take time each day to be in your body and away from your mind. Feel your feelings and check in with your heart center. This can be done through sitting or walking meditation, being in nature, yoga, or any way that you can quiet your mind and take some time to connect to your true self.

Awareness happens in the present moment.

BELIEF

Your beliefs shape your reality. Since you get to believe whatever you choose, why not choose what makes you feel the best, the most at peace with yourself and the world? Ego has a need for things to be evidence based. When we are operating out of ego, it feels hard to believe in something that we can't actually see or prove in that moment. The more we connect with our true selves through meditation or similar activities, the more we will know that we are our true selves (absolute love) and not our ego (conditioned mind).

When we know we are our true selves then we can allow ourselves to connect to our internal guidance system and be guided by the divine. We will know this is the truth because we are connected to our truth not our ego. You are a soul in a human body connected to the divine at all times, which connects you to all others. Believing you are just a human body, not connected to others or the divine, feels scary because this isn't our truth. Believing you are just a body feels isolating and overwhelming because you are not meant to manage the world on your own.

We have a choice. We can choose to believe that the world is a scary place and that we are merely a body, or we can choose to believe that we are much more than our physical bodies, more than our conditioning. That we are in fact our true selves, a soul in a human body, having a human experience. It ultimately comes down to this: Will you choose your beliefs to be based in love or fear?

Practice: Take some time to explore what beliefs feel the best for you. No one is judging you, so be honest with yourself. Choose what beliefs make you feel most happy and at peace. Why not choose to believe that our world is benevolent, that the divine is always guiding you, and that things are always working out for you? That anything is possible? Doesn't that feel better than the alternative?

WE DON'T SEE THINGS AS THEY ARE, WE SEE THINGS AS WE ARE.

- ANAIS NIN

BREATHING

Breath equals life. Your breath is a wonderful way to help you be present, to help ground you in your body. Next time you are feeling anxious or ungrounded, help yourself return to the present moment through your breath. Put one hand on your heart and one hand on your belly, and take a few moments to feel your breath coming into and out of your body. Feel your chest and belly rising and falling, and feel the weight and warmth of your hands. Then enjoy the peace and calm this brings.

Practice: Take time today to ground yourself through your breath. Anytime you notice that you are not present, take a moment to notice your breath coming in and out of your nose. Observe your chest rising and falling. Allow yourself to come back into your body, back into the present moment.

CONSCIOUSNESS

Who am I? Who is watching the one who asks, "Who am I?" Consciousness means to be awake. Aware. In this sense it means to be aware of your true self. Aware that there are two parts to you: your true self and your ego. Your true self has always loved you, always will, and is always there for you no matter what. No judgements or criticisms, just pure acceptance for who you are. It's important that you don't forget who you truly are. You are so much more than your physical body. Remember when you notice that you are judging or criticizing yourself that this isn't coming from your true self; it is coming from your ego.

Practice: Practice honoring your true self today! Listen to what your true self is asking for throughout the day and do your best to honor every request. This means practicing choosing yourself over others or situations. Notice when you have a need, such as being tired and needing to rest, rather than hanging out with a friend. We often disregard our needs because we don't want our friends to feel bad or to be mad at us. Maybe you are reaching your limit at work, but you're afraid to ask for help because you think they might fire you, so you keep slugging along doing more than you should. Begin to notice ways that you are able to honor your needs and ways in which you could use some practice choosing yourself.

COURAGE

Courage means that we can take small steps forward in spite of our fear. Fear can be a sign that we are growing. Sometimes fear keeps us safe from dangerous situations, but most often fear is our ego's way of keeping us in suffering. When we are feeling blocked by fear, we can ask ourselves, is this my ego telling me I'm not ready? If so, try speaking to yourself gently as you would to a young child. Maybe try something like this: "My dear one, I promise to keep you safe and that there is no way that you can fail." You can say this or something similar to yourself as often as you need to throughout your day.

By taking a step forward, you will only gain more knowledge about what is right or wrong for you. You will learn more about what feels good and what doesn't. Anything that doesn't work out as you were expecting is an opportunity for new growth, so it's not a failure—it's a door opening.

Practice: What is one way that you can be more courageous in your life? Maybe you have been wanting to talk to someone new at work, or you've been wanting to tell your partner you're not happy. Perhaps you want to apply for grad school or a new job. Can you take one small step toward creating the life you want for yourself? Maybe it's simply going to the school and getting the application or agreeing to go to an event that the new coworker will be at. One step can be small. It doesn't have to mean you are going to decide to follow this through; you are just checking it out to see how it feels. If you like the first step, then you can take another. Anything is possible one step at a time. Make sure your steps feel really easy and manageable, and remind yourself that you only have to focus on that one step right now. You'll focus on the next one when you get to it.

CREATIVITY

Every child is an artist. The problem is how to remain an artist once he grows up.
—Pablo Picasso

Creativity is something we all have within ourselves. Getting in touch with this aspect of ourselves is key to living an emboldened life. The first step is to declare yourself creative. The next step is to begin to honor your unique creativity. How do you do this? Begin to listen to your true self to understand what being creative looks like for you. Another way of saying this is to look for what brings you joy. What sort of activities or encounters activate joy and excitement for you? Maybe it's painting or collaging. Or maybe you feel a certain thrill when you are journaling or gardening. My brain enjoys coming up with solutions to difficult problems that are outside the box. If I didn't allow myself to be creative, I might not be able to come up with some of the zany ideas that I do. When you feel joy and excitement, you know you are headed in the right direction. Creativity also requires trusting yourself because being creative is courageous. Being creative means you are allowing yourself to be unique. You are taking a step outside the norm to express what is true for you personally, based on your own experiences.

It makes sense that the creative aspect of ourselves might get stifled with conditioning. It can be dangerous to go against the stream in our world. We may shut down our creativity in order to keep ourselves safe by blending in with everyone else. As you go through this process of getting more in touch with your true self, you will have the opportunity to get more in touch with your own creativity. This will allow you to see how you might begin to take steps toward the life you desire. Often getting where we want to go in life requires us to think outside the box, which is being creative. This requires that we trust ourselves, not what others will think.

Practice: Try to find a way to be creative each and every day. What sorts of things generate joy and excitement for you? When you have ideas, don't immediately shut them down. For example, if you feel drawn to signing up for an art class or paint night, don't talk yourself out of it because you "are not artistic." Allow yourself to play around with those ideas. Remember, anything is possible. It is only your thinking that makes it otherwise.

DHARMA

Dharma is your life's purpose. Your dharma may not be synonymous with the work you do to make money. It can be separate, although for some people it is the same. In order to find your life's purpose, you need to be in touch with your true self. If you learn to listen to your true self, it will guide you where you need to go. You can trust yourself. Follow your heart. Often our ego keeps us from our purpose, making us think that our work can't be easy or fun—that it's not really work and we can't possibly make money if it brings us joy. This is the opposite of the truth. If you follow your joy and it feels easy, you're right where you need to be, and the money will follow.

Practice: Complete the following statements:

1. I feel most at ease when I am doing _____.
2. The things I love to do the most in my life are _____.
3. The following activities bring me joy: _____.

Take a look at your three statements and think about how you can begin incorporating these activities into your life more frequently. Engaging in these activities is enough to help you understand how they should fit into your life. Maybe one of these things is meant to be your career, or you'll realize that doing these things on a regular basis really adds to your quality of life.

DIGNITY

Dignity means to be worthy of honor and respect. Everyone in this entire universe deserves dignity, including you. When we have lost our connection with our true self, we lose our sense of dignity. Remember, your true self is always there. It never disappears; it simply gets covered up by ego. You will notice as you travel throughout the world how many people have lost their sense of dignity. We can make a real difference in our world by practicing dignity. Help to restore others' dignity by acknowledging their presence, helping them to know that they matter. The next time you pass by someone suffering, don't just pass by because it's too painful. Look that person in the eye and smile. Everyone deserves love and acknowledgment.

Practice: Practice dignity today. Help yourself and others remember who you truly are. You deserve to be honored and respected! This could be as simple as making eye contact and smiling at others as you pass by them. This acknowledges their presence and thereby their worth. Or it could be helping out a friend or coworker who is struggling with his or her current circumstances. You can remind your friends that their external circumstances do not get to determine their worth. They are lovable and worthy, even if things aren't going well at work or in their personal lives. You can do the same for yourself, or maybe you need to set boundaries with others in order to take care of yourself. People will treat you how you allow them to, and you deserve to be treated with respect. Take some time to explore this for yourself and see if you can begin to take steps toward acting with dignity for yourself and others.

EGO (Conditioned Self)

Your conditioning from the outside world develops your ego. Your ego is based in fear and is developed as a form of protection from the outside world. You will not be free from ego by rejection, hate, avoidance, or any other negative stance. Integration and freedom from ego will only come through love and acceptance. Ego is a part of your true self, and only through understanding and nurturance will you find the freedom from ego that you seek.

Practice: Imagine taking your ego out of your body and sitting her next to you on the couch. Would this person be someone you want to spend all your time with? Could you be best friends with her? Would you be okay with how she spoke to you? If not, then what kind of person would be your best friend? Who would you want to spend 24 hours a day with? Think about this because this is your reality. Work to treat yourself in a way that you would want a best friend to treat you. Practice awareness, and when your ego is being unkind, take time to chat with her. Ask her why she is being unkind. What would make her feel better right now? More safe? More loved? Maybe she might like to go for a walk or grab an ice cream? Let her know that you love her! That she is so lovely and lovable. That she deserves nothing but the best.

ENERGY

We experience many different feelings throughout the day. I think it's helpful if we think of our emotions as energy. All energy is really the same. The energy simply must be felt and then it can be released from our body. Our conditioning is such that we have learned that pain is bad and should be avoided, but we can train ourselves to be okay with whatever arises. We can learn that pain is tolerable and that it can help us grow. If we don't feel our feelings, they get trapped in our body and this will eventually wreak havoc in some way. Often, it comes out in the form of anxiety or depression. Unfelt feelings are taking up space that we could be using to enhance our well-being instead of making us suffer. Wouldn't you rather use that space for love and creativity?

On the flip side, joy, happiness, and feeling good are great, but these don't last either. Clinging to these emotions also causes suffering. We can feel these amazing feelings and practice letting them go. We are ideally aiming for contentment, or the middle way. This means we know we will be okay whether things are good or bad, because we get to control how we feel about whatever comes our way.

Practice: Practice feeling all emotions as they arise. Tell yourself that pain is the same as any other energy and that you can learn to tolerate pain through practice. We need to feel in order to heal. When we avoid feeling pain, we are not escaping it; we are only prolonging it.

ENLIGHTENMENT

Enlightenment is when you are able to gain awareness of and connection to your true self and an understanding of how to operate from this place in the world. Enlightenment is something that most people believe to be unattainable, but this is not true. Awareness and enlightenment are simply fleeting, so be patient with yourself and enjoy the moments when you are aware. You are human, so you will continue to go in and out of being aware. You will have times when you get sucked into ego and times when you react in ways that are not as you would like. This doesn't mean you are no longer aware or that you're not spiritual. It likely means there is a part of you that is still healing and is acting up in order to attract your attention. Even when you don't act out, certain situations will still trigger you, annoy you, and so on. Just because you become aware or enlightened doesn't mean the world ceases to have annoyances, but how you are able to handle the annoyances shifts.

Practice: Notice how you are in the world during the times when you feel annoyed or triggered. Has your ability to handle these situations shifted? Wherever you are with it is okay! You are exactly where you need to be. Practice soothing yourself and reminding yourself that peace is an inside job.

FAITH

If you knew who walked beside you at all times, on the path that you have chosen, you could never experience fear or doubt again.
—Wayne W. Dyer

Research has shown again and again that those people who have faith in something more than their physical bodies, such as a soul, divine energy, or God, report being happier than those who don't. We get busy with our lives, and we don't realize how much the world is conspiring to help us. If you pay attention, you will see that this is true.

A nice practice to help you see this is to take time each day to write down the things that went well for you or helped you to move toward where you want to go. The world works in mysterious ways, and if we are not paying attention, we might miss the cues or the help that is right in front of us. Often things don't work out as we expected, but there is always something to be learned. You can ask yourself, *what do I need to learn from this?* Practice trusting that things are working out just as they should. Have faith that everything is in perfect order and that the world is looking out for you.

Practice: Take time each day to write down the things that went well for you or helped you to move toward where you want to go.

FEAR

It is usually pretty easy to differentiate between the fear that is related to danger and the fear that is afraid of growth. Is it our ego or our true self speaking to us? If our true self is speaking then the fear may be a warning in order to keep us safe, but if it is our ego speaking then it is likely not being helpful. The more you practice being in touch with your true self, the easier it will be to differentiate between the two.

Fear is usually your ego speaking to you. It is trying to keep you safe, but listening to this fear will often keep you stuck in unhappy situations. Fear can also be a sign of growth. It can mean that you are pushing right up on your limits, and if you keep moving, in spite of your fear, you'll soon have growth. Another way to look at fear is that you are in the process of trying to grow. Phrasing it this way feels much better than saying, *I'm too scared to do this* or *change is too hard.* You can do it in spite of the fear. We can't grow without fear, so the absence of fear means you aren't growing. The more you practice being comfortable with fear, the easier it gets. Remember that you are in great company. No one who does anything great is free from fear.

Practice: Are there any aspects of your life where you are experiencing fear? Write down everything that comes to mind about this fear. What does your fear need to hear from you? What would help you to feel more safe? See if there is one small step that you can take in spite of your fear.

FORGIVENESS

Forgiveness is really all about you. Holding on to feelings such as anger, resentment, and pain only hurts you. Forgiveness is taking care of yourself by releasing these negative emotions. I think there are two elements to forgiveness:

1. Self-love and acceptance – When we know our worth, it is easier for us to forgive, because our worth isn't wrapped up in getting our needs met by whomever we need to forgive. We know we are enough, we know that we are not alone, and so we can let go in love. Forgiveness doesn't mean the actions of another are okay or that you have to forget. It also doesn't mean that this person has to be in your life. Sometimes it isn't safe for us to have certain people in our lives, but we can still forgive them and free up the negative energy that is having a negative effect on our bodies and on our lives. We can forgive people without ever having to see them or speak to them. You are also included in forgiveness. Often we need our own forgiveness the most.

2. Empathy – The second aspect of forgiveness is understanding that the people who hurt you (including yourself) likely didn't have the skills to love you properly. They are acting from their own conditioning and are lacking those things for themselves as well. Remember that we can't give what we don't have. This understanding can help in letting go and being able to forgive.

Practice: Forgiveness meditation: Take time to think about whom you need to forgive. Maybe it's yourself. Rate whomever you need to forgive on a scale from 1 to 10, with 1 being more unwilling to forgive and 10 being complete forgiveness. How much are you willing to forgive this person or yourself in this moment? Go with your initial gut reaction. Now take some time to utilize empathy and to understand why this person might have acted the way he or she did. Maybe he was really struggling in his life or maybe she lacks the skills due to the conditioning she received as a child? Then ask yourself what you would now rate this person on the forgiveness scale from 1 to 10. Has it shifted at all? Do this every day until you reach 10.

As part of forgiveness you can also practice Ho'oponopono or the self-love exercises mentioned on page 34.

GRATITUDE

Being grateful helps to remind you that things are working for you, and it creates more of what you're grateful for. It feels good to be grateful, and it feels bad to focus on what isn't working for you. What you focus on becomes your reality. The world acts like a mirror in this regard. When you are thinking and feeling that things are not working for you then you are in a state of fear and lack. This makes the external world feel scary and lacking. When you are grateful, you are open and in a space where you believe that things can work in your favor. This makes you feel that the world is benevolent and on your side, and it creates a feeling of worthiness within you. Feeling worthy makes you feel lovable, so gratitude is a great step on the path to self-love.

Practice: Begin each morning and end each evening in gratitude. Think of all the things that you are grateful for no matter how small. You may only be able to think of one or two things to begin with, but the more you do it, the more you will notice all that you have to be grateful for. I am grateful for my health, my able body, my home, my family, my cozy bed, my sobriety, my job, my abundance, my animals, my friends, the life I've created, my opportunities, the sunshine, nature, love, God, travel, and so on and so on.

HAPPINESS

Happiness is a choice. We must decide each day upon waking whether we will be happy or not. Then we must practice happiness. Knowing that happiness is a choice means that we can be happy each day, regardless of what life presents to us. We may not have control over what happens to us externally, but we do have control over what happens internally. I know this may seem hard to believe, but we really can learn to be okay and choose to be happy no matter what is happening around us.

This doesn't mean that we stuff our feelings; it means that a difficult situation doesn't have to ruin our day or make us grumpy. It means we acknowledge how we are feeling and attend to ourselves in a loving way, knowing that becoming grumpy or defeated won't help the situation or move it forward. We are human, so of course we will still feel grumpy or defeated at times, but the more we practice sitting with our emotions and accepting what is, the less this will happen. Circumstances never remain the same. We will have difficulties but they won't last forever, and we will have lots of joy but that also won't last forever. Knowing this can be helpful, especially when we are in the midst of a difficult situation. We can relax knowing that this too shall pass.

Practice: Upon waking each day, say to yourself, "This is going to be the best day of my life! I choose to be happy, regardless of what I encounter today." Do you notice as you begin to make a practice of this how your overall attitude changes?

HEALTH

How you take care of yourself is a sign of self-love. The more you grow to love yourself, the kinder you will treat yourself and the healthier you will become. When you love yourself, you will not want to cause yourself harm. Are there ways in which you are currently causing yourself harm? Take some time to think about the choices you are currently making for your health. This includes what you put into your body and how you treat your body. Are you eating healthy, exercising, getting enough sleep, avoiding intoxicants, and taking time to connect with your true self through meditation, nature, or yoga?

Practice: See if you can make more loving choices for your health this week. Is there one area of your life where you can begin to be more loving toward yourself? When you have the urge to engage in harmful behavior, such as intoxicants or overeating, check in to see what this behavior is really about. What do you really need? Are you actually just tired and needing rest? Could you be disappointed or sad and in need of some nurturing attention?

HO'OPONOPONO

This is a Hawaiian forgiveness ritual. You can use this for yourself or others any time you feel that things are out of balance or lacking in peace. Here are the simple steps.

Say each of these four sentences while imagining the person you need to forgive:

1. I'm sorry. (This is about being sorry for bringing yourself or another into suffering.)
2. I forgive you. (This means that you forgive whomever or yourself for the suffering you have endured and caused or that they caused you.)
3. I love you. (You love this person unconditionally and despite anything that has happened.)
4. Thank you. (You acknowledge that these actions are already taking place.)

You can say this in meditation or throughout your day. If you are working on self-forgiveness and you'd like to experience the impact quickly, say this in the mirror 10 times a day.

Forgiveness is so powerful. Often the things we are holding onto wreak havoc on our bodies and can cause things like anxiety, depression, and many other illnesses. Forgiveness sets us free.

Practice: Practice using Ho'oponopono to work on forgiving yourself or someone else.

I AM

Your conditioning has likely created a lot of *I am not* in your thinking. *I'm not good at this, I'm not capable of doing that, I'm not that kind of person,* and so on. Remember that your inner reality shapes your outer reality. What do you want your outer reality to look like? Practice making your inner world congruent with your true self. These two words, I AM, are powerful beyond belief, so be mindful of what you place after them because this will become your truth. When you use I AM, you are defining yourself and what you're capable of. I AM is a holy expression of your true self, so use it wisely. Use I AM to honor your true self, to put you in the right frame of mind, and to create the reality that you want for yourself. Recondition yourself to realize the unlimited power of your true self.

Practice: Practice shifting *I am not* to I AM. I AM love, I AM successful, I AM abundant. I AM smart. I AM healthy. I AM happy. What resonates for you? What have you been telling yourself you're not capable of? Start there and flip the script!

INNER CHILD

Even though you've grown into an adult, your inner child still resides inside you. As children we are dependent upon the adults in our life, and if they can't meet our needs, we can't help but internalize this as something wrong with us, or our needs. As adults we tend to continue to treat our inner child as the adults treated us growing up. This will keep the inner child in a space of fear, shame, and confusion. We are not really aware of this conditioning until we get older and we start to get fed up with the suffering. This is likely when we begin to realize that we are treating ourselves unkindly. What your inner child really needs is for you to listen to her, to honor her wishes and needs, and to parent her in a way that makes her feel safe and loved. She needs to know that she is beautiful and accepted just as she is.

Practice 1: Make a list of all the things you needed to hear growing up. Most of us need to hear things like: I'm proud of you, I love you unconditionally, you are beautiful, you're doing a great job, and so on. These are the things you need to hear now. Practice saying these things to yourself whenever you need to hear them. You can also practice saying these things to yourself in the mirror, which amps up the message in a powerful way!

Practice 2: Practice listening to your inner child and meeting her needs whenever possible. Remember, acceptance is key. However she is feeling is okay. Don't make her feel bad for how she is feeling. Just try to figure out what she needs. It might sound something like this: *I'm sorry you're feeling like this. This is painful and I'm here for you. I love you. What might make you feel better right now?* Maybe give her some examples. *Would you like to take a walk? A bath? Cuddle with the cat?* Or it could sound like this: *I'm so proud of you! You did such a good job and you deserve to be happy, my love.*

INSPIRATION

Daily inspiration is important to help keep you on your path. Inspiration can come in many forms: meditation, reading books, attending workshops or conferences, being creative, or spending time with inspiring people. It looks different for everyone, but it is helpful for us to hear the same things over and over. I often read the same book many times. It is also helpful to have contact with like-minded people. If you don't already have friends who are on a similar path as you then it might be helpful to join a mastermind group or a coaching group.

Self-love and peace require practice, but this practice doesn't have to feel like work. These practices can become part of your daily routine. Hopefully, they will become like beloved friends that you can't live without.

Practice: What inspires you the most? What helps keep you on your path? How can you include more of this in your daily life? I like to meditate, listen to inspiring books, and repeat daily mantras to help keep myself on my path.

JOY

Our lives should be infused with daily spurts of joy! What brings you joy? Take a moment to write down whatever makes you feel joy. It's okay for you to be happy, and your soul is meant to feel joy. This is your birthright and your natural state of being. Joy comes in all sizes. We can find joy in the smallest things: a cup of tea, a smile, a sunset, the sun warming your back, a hug, animals, babies, and so on.

Practice: Take some time each day to write down the moments of joy you experienced throughout your day. It will bring you joy to be reminded of them.

KINDNESS

You, yourself, as much as anybody in the entire universe, deserve your love and affection.
—Unknown

It's difficult to be kind to others when you're unkind to yourself. Treat yourself as you would like someone to treat you or how you might treat a small child. What you do to others you do to yourself. This is why when you are unkind to another it feels bad. You may feel justified or good for a moment, but before long you'll be feeling bad. If for no other reason than feeling good yourself, treat others kindly. Yes, even when they've wronged you.

Practice: Practice random acts of kindness this week. Think of thoughtful acts that you or someone else might enjoy. Here are some ideas:

1. Take someone's grocery cart back for them.
2. Pay someone's bridge toll.
3. Let someone go ahead of you in line.
4. Hold the door for someone.
5. Tell someone something you like about them.
6. Bring someone flowers.
7. Bring cookies to work.

LOVE

Be still and know that I am God.
—Psalm 46:10

You are love and therefore you are divine. You and the divine are one. A separate ego-self is an illusion. When you are willing to give up your ego identity, you will know love, and you will know god.

When we are present and open, we are devoid of ego, making ourselves available to the truth, available to know God, to know love. When we tap into our true selves, we know that we are fully loved by the divine, that we are the divine. This is always there; our true nature never leaves us. It is only our ego that will question this, that will disbelieve this. When we are in anything other than love, we can know that we are disconnected from our true nature, that we are in ego. When this happens take a moment to tune back into your true self, to come back to love.

It all comes down to love. The more we love ourselves, the more we will accept ourselves, and the happier we will be. The more we love ourselves, the more we can love others. The more we love others, the more connected we feel, and the happier we are. Anything is possible with love.

Practice: Practice one or more forms of self-love daily. We need to practice loving ourselves each and every day. There are lots of great examples in this book: Mirror work, gratitude, and Ho'oponopono are all powerful tools for helping you to love yourself. Start loving yourself today!

MEDITATION

Meditation is a way for us to connect to our source (our true self). The more you connect with your true self, the easier it is to listen to this part of yourself. Your true self is your natural guidance system. This part of you knows what you need and want, and the more you honor yourself, the happier and more at peace you will be. Sometimes it's really hard for us to hear our true self, because our ego is so loud and we think that our ego is our true self (but our true self would never be unkind or critical toward us). Our true self has always loved us exactly as we are and will continue to love us no matter what.

Meditation Instruction

You may have little to no experience meditating and so may likely benefit from some basic instruction or refreshing your current knowledge. There is no right way to meditate. Meditating is a time you've set aside for yourself to listen and get to know your true self.

The Space and Sitting

Create a space for yourself where you would like to meditate. You can sit on the floor with a pillow or sit in a chair. It is important to be comfortable but also upright. Sitting upright with proper alignment will help you with your concentration and the tension on your body. It's nice to do something special like light a candle or create an altar with some meaningful objects. This helps you to feel loved and is an acknowledgment that you are special and deserve to be honored.

The Basics

Place one hand on your heart and one hand on your belly. This is useful for many reasons:

1. Your own hands and touch are very healing.
2. You can feel the warmth and weight of your hands and this is comforting and nurturing.
3. It gives you a place to bring your attention to when you need to refocus.

You will continue to have thoughts. A lot of people get really frustrated by this, but it's normal. This is where patience for yourself can come in really handy. When you notice that you are lost in your thoughts, bring your attention back to your hands and allow this to reground you. It's okay if you have to do this 100 times during a session. It's part of learning. You are teaching yourself and training your mind. Remember, you didn't learn to ride a bike on your first try!

Once you are grounded in your body, begin to notice how you are feeling. How is your heart center, your belly, and other parts of you?

Setting a Timer and Tolerance

When you meditate, you are also learning tolerance. Sometimes meditating is pleasant and sometimes it isn't. You are learning to be with yourself in all conditions. This is why setting a timer is important for a variety of reasons:

1. You won't have to worry about how much time has passed or how much time you have left.

2. You will be with yourself until the timer sounds, even if you are ready to be done. Sometimes life feels intolerable, but if you can learn to be accepting of it, and tolerant of uncomfortable and painful feelings, then you can learn to be at peace.

3. Even if you are having a good experience, it's still important

to end when the timer goes off. Again, you are learning acceptance of what is. In life we will have highs and lows. It's just as important that we don't cling to the highs as it is to not avoid the lows. This is why when you are having a joyful meditation you end when the timer rings. You can feel grateful for the positive experience but then let it go. You can reset the timer for an additional sitting session, but go into the next session with a clean slate and no expectations of what will be, and in this way you can be content with whatever arises for you.

As I mentioned earlier, start small. I usually recommend five minutes to start. This will help you establish a routine and it should feel pretty easy. Gradually, over time, work your way up to 30 minutes one to two times a day. In the scheme of things, 30 to 60 minutes out of your entire day is nothing.

Practice: Practice five minutes or more of sitting meditation. Be sure to set your timer.

MIRROR WORK

I love mirror work. Mirror work helps you to see your true self and to love yourself unconditionally. I have found it to be one of the most effective tools in my own life, and I often recommend it to my clients as well. I have discovered that it is highly effective in a short period of time, if you're diligent about doing it on a regular basis. I promise that you will see results if you do it every day.

Keep in mind that mirror work will stir up the ego, but this is part of the mirror work. As you say your mantras in the mirror, your ego may begin to speak up and say mean things like *ugh... look at your wrinkles, why does your nose look like that?* or *you're not lovable.* Just remember this is to be expected and it's not true. All you have to do is notice the ego's voice and return your focus back to your beautiful eyes and to your mantra, which will soon be your new truth.

Practice:

1. Look yourself in the eyes in the mirror.

2. Choose some mantras that resonate with you. I usually recommend coming up with a few different ones. Any of these are good options to start with:

   1) I love you.
   2) I love you so much.
   3) I am so lovable or You are so loveable.
   4) I am willing to receive love today.
   5) *Life loves me.

You can begin using I statements, but you may find it feels more comfortable to use You statements. You get to decide what feels most powerful for you. I think it's good to begin your focus on love because this is your truth, your foundation. As you become more acquainted with mirror work, you can begin to add other mantras that resonate with you, such as I am beautiful and I am so smart. You really can't go wrong as long as it resonates with you.

3. Say your chosen mantras in the mirror 10 times in a row, one to two times a day. If you've chosen more than one mantra, you will say all of them 10 different times. In the morning upon rising and in the evening before retiring is a great way to start and end your day. Remember, the more you practice the more you will benefit.

*This mantra helps you to remember that the world is benevolent and is working in your favor. It is only your own mind that tells you differently. Everything is trying to help you reach your highest, best self. Every moment and every experience is trying to help you. Even when life is hard and doesn't feel good, we are getting just what we need to learn to love ourselves unconditionally, which in turn helps us to love all others unconditionally.

Note: It is helpful to put a little reminder note on your mirror so that you won't forget. I often put sticky notes on my bathroom mirror, and when I see them I do some mirror work.

NAMASTE

I love this word and its meaning: *The light in me bows to the light in you.* It's so special. It's a nice reminder that we are all connected by the same light. Some people's light shines brighter than others due to conditioning, but this doesn't make anyone less deserving of your love. When you honor the light in another, you remind her of her own light and you strengthen yours at the same time. You can honor the light in others in very simple ways. Just a small acknowledgment will do. Look into someone's eyes, say hello and smile, or simply nod your head.

Practice: How can you honor the light in others today? Begin to think of ways that you can help others know their goodness. Sometimes it's as simple as making eye contact or physical contact with someone, such as a reassuring pat or embrace. It could be verbal reassurance of someone's goodness, or perhaps you go out of your way to help another person in order to help him know his worthiness. Like sponsoring someone for an educational endeavor or a meditation retreat. The possibilities are endless. Take some time to journal about ideas that come up for you around honoring others in this way.

OPENNESS

Openness is being open to what life has to offer. If we pay attention, we will notice that we open and close throughout the day. We also have ways of thinking or have had experiences that close us down to certain aspects of life, or sometimes everything. We close down to protect ourselves. We believe we are keeping ourselves safe, but the problem with being closed is that we are also closed to the positive things we want to experience as well. For example, if we believe we have been hurt by love and we decide to shut ourselves off from love in order to keep from being hurt again then when love comes along we won't be open to receive it. Remember, love actually never hurt us in the first place. It was anything other than love that hurt us. Love can never hurt us.

We are always safe with love. Sometimes we might be closed to love because we are reserving it for the "right" person, or maybe we are afraid to be loving to everyone because we don't want to give people the "wrong" idea. Any of these ways we are closing only keep us from love because we are not open to receive it. We can love freely, knowing we can trust ourselves to manage any situation that presents itself. Remember, love cannot hurt you, so when anything arises other than love, you will know what you need to do in that moment. We always have everything we need to manage any situation in the present moment.

Practice: Throughout the day practice being aware of whether you are open or closed to love. Another way to say this is: Is your heart open or closed? What do you notice that helps your heart open? What do you notice that makes it close? See if you can practice remaining open when you feel inclined to close. Please be gentle with the part of you that wants to close. Let this part of you know that she is safe—that love can't hurt her, that she has everything she needs to keep herself safe.

PAIN

Pain is a feeling like any other, and we can learn to be with our pain. Learn to sit with it and tolerate its presence. We are often scared to feel our pain so we avoid it, thereby trapping it in our bodies, saving it for another time. As I've mentioned before, we will not avoid it forever—it will eventually surface in some form. The more we practice being with our pain, the easier it becomes. We can learn that it is an energy like any other. We can feel it and allow it to exit our bodies. Sometimes we think that we don't have control over our emotions, but this is not true. We can learn to be with our pain and learn to soothe ourselves so that our pain doesn't have to impact others.

Practice: The next time you encounter painful feelings, see if you can be present with them. Allow yourself to feel your pain, thereby allowing it to dissipate. Practice soothing yourself rather than letting your pain project onto someone else. When you notice you are triggered in some way, rather than snapping at your partner, or being impatient with the checkout person at the grocery store, try going inward and see what sort of soothing you may need. Perhaps you are hungry, overwhelmed, or sad? The first step is to understand how you are feeling and then you can practice understanding what it is you need when you are feeling that way. Do you need to stop and get something to eat, or take a break and have a moment of quiet? The more you practice attending to yourself, the easier it will become.

PEACE

Peace. It does not mean to be in a place where there is no noise, trouble or hard work. It means to be in the midst of those things and still be calm in your heart.
—Unknown

Peace means feeling at ease, regardless of what is happening around you. Meditation is extremely helpful in teaching us peace. Meditation teaches us tolerance for what is and how to be okay and accepting of ourselves in all circumstances. What we learn in meditation translates to life, and this is how we learn to be at peace no matter what we are facing externally. We don't have control of the external, but we always have control of our internal circumstances.

Practice: Practice being at peace in your body today, regardless of what you are facing externally. I find it helpful to focus on my heart center when I need to find peace in my body. I focus on feeling my heart and allow the love I feel to radiate out to the rest of my body. Placing a hand on your heart can aid in this process.

PRACTICING

To change your life, to change your current ways of being, takes practice. There is no avoiding this. *You must practice.* I promise you that if you practice, you will see change. If you do not wish to change, or you have not reached your tolerance for suffering, then you can keep doing things exactly as you have been. I find that if you develop daily rituals it can be helpful in practicing and creating habits. Little reminders are also helpful. Sticky notes on the mirror, your meditation pillow in a place where you often walk by, or a community that you meet to do group practice are all helpful examples. Most important is finding what works best for you in order to maintain a daily practice.

Practice: Take some time to journal about the changes you would like to see in your life. What types of practices have you explored that could be helpful with these changes? What practices have resonated the most for you? Make a list of the practices that you would like to engage in on a regular basis. How can you begin to implement these practices into your daily life? What form of practice will you engage in today?

PRESENCE

Being present is an important part of a spiritual practice. If we are in the future, we likely feel anxious because the unknown is out of our control and that feels scary. We can plan for the future from the present when it is necessary, but worrying about the future isn't helpful. We think that ruminating about how things will turn out in the future will help us to prepare, but things don't usually unfold the way we expect them to, and we waste our precious energy on feelings of anxiety around worst-case scenarios that may never occur. We can handle anything that comes to us in the present.

If we are dwelling in the past, we are likely feeling depressed. We can't change the past; we can only learn from it. Beating ourselves up about it only makes us feel bad. It doesn't change anything. If you want to do things differently, that's fine, but that doesn't mean you have to beat yourself up about it. Start in the present moment. Each moment is a new opportunity. The present moment is the only place we are truly free. If we are in the future or in the past, we are missing what is happening in this moment.

Practice: Here are some questions to ask yourself when you notice that you are not in the present moment that will allow you to come back to the present:

1. Is there anything wrong in this moment?
2. Is there any action that I can take?

Sometimes we are worrying about things we need to do, so maybe we can make a list or take another action like make a phone call. If you cannot take action then you can let go of whatever is worrying you, knowing that everything is okay in this moment and that there are no actions that you can currently take.

Awareness happens in the present moment

QUIET

Quiet the mind so that you can hear your soul speak. Take time to sit in quiet so that you can feel the love and energy emanating from within. Our lives tend to be so busy that we forget to take the time to renew and rejuvenate our souls. It doesn't have to be through meditation. You can do this by being in nature, practicing yoga, or anything that allows you to hear and feel your inner stillness. You deserve this gift for yourself.

Practice: How will you practice inner stillness today? Perhaps you already have a meditation practice and you want to practice siting on your own, or maybe you don't and you want to try meditating for the first time? Would you prefer to go out into nature to experience the power of silence amongst the trees and plants? Or would you rather be part of a community by taking a group yoga or qigong class? Take a moment to explore how you'd like to experience inner stillness today!

"Tell me, what is it you plan to do with your one wild and precious life?" Mary Oliver

RECEIVE

Sometimes it can be hard to receive—and this can keep us from having abundance and love in our lives. It can be scary and vulnerable to open ourselves up to receive, especially if we've been hurt. But I want to remind you that love has never hurt you. Anything but love may have hurt you in the past but love will never hurt you.

There are many ways we can receive each day. Pay attention and begin to practice receiving. Remember that it is just as beneficial to the giver as it is to the receiver. Go ahead and receive with gratitude. You can receive through a compliment, someone opening a door for you, a smile, a laugh, a hug, a meal, guidance, love, kindness, and so on.

Practice: Try this mantra: I am willing to receive today! Say it as often as you can throughout the day. Then see how the opportunities to receive show up in your life.

RESPECT

When we love ourselves, we know our worth. When we know our worth, we won't settle for less than what we deserve. We won't allow others to disrespect us or treat us unkindly. The more we love ourselves, the more easily we can love others. Loving yourself and others is all the same love. Knowing this can help us to understand that what we do for ourselves impacts others and what we do to others also impacts us.

Practice: Practice showing yourself and others respect today. Here is a list of examples for you to explore. Choose one or more of the examples from the list to put into practice today.

1. Listen—truly listening is validating.
2. Be thankful for the support and assistance that others show you.
3. Affirm—affirming others makes them feel that what they are saying or doing matters.
4. Encourage—help someone to know he is capable and that you respect his abilities.
5. Congratulate—celebrate someone's ability or achievement.
6. Be helpful—helping without being asked shows a great deal of respect.

SELF-LOVE

Self-Love is what this book is all about—ways to learn to love yourself, and to have more compassion and acceptance for yourself. The reason it feels so hard to love ourselves is because of our ego. We have been conditioned to think and believe in a certain way. A majority of the time this is negative thinking or judgements against ourselves. As we begin to be more loving it can feel inauthentic, and our ego will likely argue with us and ramp up the negativity. We are truly reprogramming our minds to be more loving, and this takes awareness, time, and practice. Please be patient with yourself.

Practice: As a first step begin to be aware of what your thoughts are on a more regular basis. Especially when you are feeling bad in your body. Use this as an opportunity to check in with yourself around why you are feeling bad. What were you thinking? Then begin utilizing daily practices to help retrain your brain—practices such as mantras, mirror work, and getting in touch with your true self through meditation. The more in touch we are with our true loving nature, the easier it is to love ourselves. It is only our mind/ego that ever makes us believe anything otherwise.

TRUST

The mind is like water. When it's turbulent, it's difficult to
see. When it's calm, everything becomes clear.
—Prasad Mahes

Trust your inner guidance or true self to guide you. Do not rely
on your thinking alone. You are exactly where you need to be
and are headed exactly where you need to be going, in order to
reach your highest, best self. This means that you can trust that
you are being guided in the right ways. If you are confused then
you need to be patient until you are clear. Think of this as you
would a turbulent pond: As it stills it becomes clear. If we are
patient with ourselves, the answers will come. Identifying with
our minds or ego will make us feel confused. Be still and listen.

Practice: Try these mantras:

I am willing to let the universe guide me today.
I trust that the right opportunities will present themselves.

Say them as often as you can throughout the day.

TRUTH

Truth is a part of honoring your soul. If you are lying to yourself or others, it is blocking your true nature, and if this continues it will build up in your body until your body acts out in a way that will get your attention. It most often looks like anxiety, and if you continue to ignore yourself then depression will likely set in over the anxiety. Truth is also about honoring what you like or dislike, how someone treats you, and speaking up for yourself. It can be as simple as voicing your preference to a friend about which restaurant you prefer.

When you don't listen to yourself, you are telling yourself that you don't matter. This is most likely continued abuse or neglect that you learned from your family of origin. The only way this will change and heal is if you begin to listen to and honor your true self, which means beginning to parent yourself in the way you wish you had been. Be the best friend you've never had. We need to be heard in order to live our truth.

Practice: As you go throughout your day, practice knowing your truths and do your best to honor them for yourself and others. Being dishonest with others isn't helping them. You may think you're saving their feelings or avoiding conflict, but likely you're keeping them from growing in ways they need. We can tell people anything in a loving way, and if someone doesn't like what we have to say or doesn't agree with us, this doesn't mean that there is anything wrong with our needs. Another person doesn't have to agree with us for our need to be valid.

UNIQUE

Each and every one of us is unique. No one is like you, and no one has the same perspective. Your experiences and innate personality give you your own unique perspective. Our conditioning, which comes from our experiences, impacts how we see things, and this is true for everyone. Everyone you meet is coming from their own personal perspective. This is why it is so important that we don't compare ourselves to others—or take on the opinions and judgements of others as our own truth. It isn't our truth; it is their truth.

Practice: The next time you notice yourself comparing your life to someone else's life, take a moment to remind yourself that you are unique. Allow yourself to appreciate your own loveliness. It's okay to be different. Just imagine what our world would be like if we were all the same. Pretty dang boring. Embrace your differences. It's what makes you beautiful!

VACATION

Music is the space between the notes.
—Claude Debussy

Taking breaks is important. Sometimes it's the space that will allow us the clarity we seek. The space between the notes is what makes the music. This doesn't mean you have to do something spectacular like leaving the country; do what your budget affords. Take time as often as you can to just be, and enjoy your free time. It could be as simple as taking yourself out to breakfast. The more you learn to do this, the easier it will be to do on a regular basis, without even taking an official break.

Practice: Take yourself out for coffee or breakfast. Allow yourself to thoroughly enjoy the time. Savor your coffee and being served. Read your book, write in your journal, and enjoy the time with yourself.

VARIETY

Variety is really important because too much routine can become boring and cause us to disengage from activities—or even life. Stability is important but not at the cost of losing variety in your life. Losing variety can make us feel stagnant and unfulfilled. Variety helps to keep you engaged and adds freshness to your life, making things seem exciting. The key to creating variety is that you have to plan it, otherwise you will instinctively go back to what you're used to. As humans we are creatures of habit.

How might you switch things up a bit in your life? What's something you'd like to try that you've never done before? Do something new each week. It can be as simple as exploring a new restaurant or attempting a new hobby or as adventurous as traveling to a new country or expanding your social circle. This will keep life stimulating and exciting. I know it can be hard to step outside your comfort zone, but you can do it one step at a time. You'll be surprised how much it adds to your life. Try it!

Practice: Choose one new activity you can add to your life this week. Maybe you've been considering learning to knit or taking a yoga class. Try it this week and see what you think. You don't have to go back if you don't like it, but you might love it, and you might meet some fabulous new people.

VOICE

Listen to your inner voice. Learning to listen to your inner voice or intuition and then honoring it is your path to freedom and happiness. Sometimes it might feel hard or even seem impossible to do what your inner voice requests, such as changing jobs, leaving a relationship, moving cities, or starting your own business. You don't have to take the next 40 steps right now, just one step. Any step toward where you want to go gets you closer.

Remember that sometimes we are over identified with our ego, and this makes it hard to hear our inner voice or even recognize it. This is why we must practice each day being close to our true self with meditation.

Practice: Aim for five to 30 minutes of meditation, connecting with your true self. Follow it up with some journaling about what your inner voice is calling you to do. What is one step that you can take toward making this happen?

WALKING MEDITATION

A walking meditation can be a nice alternative or addition to sitting meditation. It is easier for us to be out of our minds when we are fully in our bodies, and an activity like walking can really help.

Introduction to Walking Meditation

You can choose to do this anywhere, but choosing a place you find pleasing to the senses is most ideal. To begin, choose a spot a little ways in the distance like a tree or a house. As you walk you can focus on that spot, while noticing how it feels in your body to be walking on the Earth. How the air, wind, or rain feels on your skin. What do you hear? Birds? Traffic? Wind? Are you cold? Warm? Is the sun shining on you? How does all of that make you feel? Peaceful? Anxious?

When you reach the point that you chose, choose a new point and begin again. Do this as long and as often as you would like. You don't have to choose focus points but you may find it helpful.

Practice: Try out walking meditation and see if it's something that you'd like to add as a regular practice for yourself.

WATER

Water is incredibly healing and cleansing for your energy. It is a soothing way to wash the day away and refresh yourself energetically. You can do this by taking a bath or shower at home or by going into nature and utilizing a river, lake, or ocean. Notice how you feel before and after going into the water. If you'd like, you can add a special element to your bath, such as salts or essential oils. This can become an act of self-care that you can add to your day.

Practice: Next time you're feeling overwhelmed by your day or an experience with someone, try taking a bath or shower and notice how this changes your energy.

WILLINGNESS

You only need to be willing for things to begin to change. What does it mean to be willing? It means you don't have to know all of the details of how something will unfold. You just have to be open to trying. This is the key to change. This will allow you to take that one step and then the next step will become apparent, and before you know it you'll be doing exactly what you set out to do.

Practice: What is one thing you want for yourself? How can you allow yourself to be more willing? What is one step you can take toward creating what you want for yourself? Resolve to take that one step this week.

XOXOX

We all need more love, not less. Especially when we are struggling or hurting. This is when we need to be the most kind and loving toward ourselves. When you act in ways that you don't like, think of this as a part of you showing up because it needs your love and attention. For example, it may feel really bad if you lose your temper with someone, but if you approach yourself from a place of acceptance instead of contempt, you can begin to understand this behavior rather than continuing it. We need to try to figure out what we need in that moment and to feel understood for our needs to be met. If we approach ourselves with contempt or anger, this aspect of ourselves will continue to surface. Acceptance is key. Once this aspect of yourself feels accepted and is able to get her needs met, she will no longer need to reappear.

Practice: The next time you exhibit behavior that you don't like, practice being accepting rather than being upset with yourself. Try to see if you can understand where the behavior originated. Was it a buildup of not being heard and you finally reached your limit, or were you feeling deprived in some way and felt you needed this behavior to feel more nurtured? There is always a reason for our behavior. We are not bad, lazy, or some other negative adjective but just trying to get our needs met, and if we listen we can begin to learn what it is that we really need in any given situation.

X-RAY VISION

Eyes are the door to the soul. You'll notice if you pay attention that people's eyes have something to say. Clear bright eyes are a sign of health. You can also see wisdom, wonder, and pain. You can help to remind others of their light, and their dignity, by looking into their eyes and acknowledging them and their light within. They will see your light and this will feel good to them because they are being reminded of their own internal light.

Practice: Honor someone else's light and dignity today by looking that person in the eyes and acknowledging him or her. You can do this at any time throughout your day, as you're passing someone on the street or checking out at the grocery store.

you are magic

YOGA

Yoga is a great way to practice mindfulness. The poses require you to be really grounded in your body and focused on your breathing. If sitting meditation is hard for you, yoga can be a nice place to start. It can help prepare your mind for sitting meditation. It's easier for us to be out of our minds and in our bodies when we are doing something that requires concentration, such as yoga.

Practice: Try taking a yoga class this week. Really focus on being mindful and in your body. When your mind starts to wander during a pose, bring it back to your body and your breath. There are many great introductory offers out there for people new to a studio and there are also online videos that you can do in the comfort of your own home. Take advantage of that to introduce yourself to yoga or to become reacquainted with the practice.

ZEN

Practice being Zen in everyday moments. You can practice mindfulness while you are doing routine activities, such as brushing your teeth, washing the dishes, or cleaning the house. While you're brushing your teeth say to yourself, *I am brushing my teeth,* and really focus on brushing your teeth and what the experience is like for you. When you are folding laundry, pay attention to each aspect of folding your clothes, or sweeping the floor, and so on. When your mind begins to wander, bring it back to what you are doing. Normally, your mind would likely be elsewhere when doing such activities, but you can practice being Zen by being completely present in these moments instead. You can do this with any activity. This can really help you practice being more present in the world. The more you meditate, the easier it will be to be present.

Practice: Choose an everyday activity like brushing your teeth or sweeping to practice being Zen today.

ZEST

Have a zest for life. Be open. You never know what will work for you or who you might connect with. If you are excited and curious then life will never be dull. Remember, you always have a choice and you can always try new things. This means that you are never trapped or stuck.

Practice: Practice being zesty today!! Have you been curious about certain things but have dismissed them as silly or useless? Try engaging in one of those activities that once peaked your interest but you dismissed in some way. Why not? Sign up for a tarot card reading or participate in a bowling league with your coworkers. Go ahead and read your horoscope today! Who cares if your ego thinks it's silly? You might discover something important or useful. You never know.

Keeping the Awareness You've Cultivated

I believe the key to staying awake and on the path free from suffering is practice. Practice daily meditation and being aware throughout your day. Awareness requires you to be present. If you are worrying about the future or ruminating about the past then you cannot be in the present. When you notice that you are caught in your thoughts, you can bring yourself back to the present moment. Just like in meditation you can do this repeatedly as you are learning.

Now that you can recognize the difference between your ego (conditioned self) and your true self (unconditioned self), you can also observe who's in charge throughout your day. Practice noticing the kinds of thoughts you are having and how they make you feel. If you are feeling bad, the ego is at work. As soon as you notice that you are feeling bad, stop yourself, and say, "I want to feel good." Then ask yourself, "What would make me feel good right now?"

When you hear your true self talking, practice honoring what this part of you wants and needs whenever possible. Keep in mind this may cause your ego to kick in and start telling you all the reasons why you shouldn't meet these needs. This is to be expected. There is a reason you weren't able to meet these needs in the first place. Whenever we are learning a new way of being, it takes time for it to feel comfortable. In the beginning it can feel awkward and inauthentic, but over time the new way of being will begin to feel comfortable, and the old way of being will be the odd one out. The more you engage in the awarenesses and practices within this book, the closer you will feel to your true self and the better you will be able listen to this part of you. Soon, with continued practice, you'll be living the life you deserve, creating happiness one letter at a time.

Acknowledgments

I am so grateful to all the lovely people who are willing to show up to do the courageous work of reconnecting with their true selves in order to gain freedom from the conditioned mind. In doing so you are helping to make the world a better place. A huge thank you to my mastermind group—Kaira West, Melissa Wright and Jonathan Logan for your ongoing inspiration and support. My editor Lara Asher and coaches Sarah Dimeo and Sarah Given who are rock stars and were beyond helpful with this entire process. My daughter, Olivia Grace, for her patience and artistic talents, and to everyone who was willing to read my manuscript in its initial stages. You all helped my dream to become a reality.

About the Author

Stephani Grace is a state-licensed and board-certified professional counselor with 21 years of experience counseling individuals and couples using her unique blend of psychology and spirituality. She specializes in the treatment of adults struggling with anxiety, depression, and weight loss. She received her BA in Psychology and MA in Counseling Psychology from Humboldt State University. She has a successful private practice in Portland, Oregon where she lives with her daughter, Olivia, her dog, Lulu, and her cats, Birdie and Gus.

O-BOOKS

SPIRITUALITY

O is a symbol of the world, of oneness and unity; this eye represents knowledge and insight. We publish titles on general spirituality and living a spiritual life. We aim to inform and help you on your own journey in this life.
If you have enjoyed this book, why not tell other readers by posting a review on your preferred book site?

Recent bestsellers from O-Books are:

Heart of Tantric Sex
Diana Richardson
Revealing Eastern secrets of deep love and intimacy to Western couples.
Paperback: 978-1-90381-637-0 ebook: 978-1-84694-637-0

Crystal Prescriptions
The A-Z guide to over 1,200 symptoms and their healing crystals
Judy Hall
The first in the popular series of eight books, this handy little guide is packed as tight as a pill-bottle with crystal remedies for ailments.
Paperback: 978-1-90504-740-6 ebook: 978-1-84694-629-5

Take Me To Truth
Undoing the Ego
Nouk Sanchez, Tomas Vieira
The best-selling step-by-step book on shedding the Ego, using the teachings of *A Course In Miracles*.
Paperback: 978-1-84694-050-7 ebook: 978-1-84694-654-7

The 7 Myths about Love...Actually!
The Journey from your HEAD to the HEART of your SOUL
Mike George
Smashes all the myths about LOVE.
Paperback: 978-1-84694-288-4 ebook: 978-1-84694-682-0

The Holy Spirit's Interpretation of the New Testament
A Course in Understanding and Acceptance
Regina Dawn Akers
Following on from the strength of *A Course In Miracles*, NTI
teaches us how to experience the love and oneness of God.
Paperback: 978-1-84694-085-9 ebook: 978-1-78099-083-5

The Message of A Course In Miracles
A translation of the Text in plain language
Elizabeth A. Cronkhite
A translation of *A Course in Miracles* into plain, everyday
language for anyone seeking inner peace. The companion
volume, *Practicing A Course In Miracles*, offers practical lessons
and mentoring.
Paperback: 978-1-84694-319-5 ebook: 978-1-84694-642-4

Your Simple Path
Find Happiness in every step
Ian Tucker
A guide to helping us reconnect with what is really important in
our lives.
Paperback: 978-1-78279-349-6 ebook: 978-1-78279-348-9

365 Days of Wisdom
Daily Messages To Inspire You Through The Year
Dadi Janki
Daily messages which cool the mind, warm the heart and guide
you along your journey.
Paperback: 978-1-84694-863-3 ebook: 978-1-84694-864-0

Body of Wisdom
Women's Spiritual Power and How it Serves
Hilary Hart
Bringing together the dreams and experiences of women across
the world with today's most visionary spiritual teachers.
Paperback: 978-1-78099-696-7 ebook: 978-1-78099-695-0

Dying to Be Free
From Enforced Secrecy to Near Death to True Transformation
Hannah Robinson
After an unexpected accident and near-death experience, Hannah
Robinson found herself radically transforming her life, while a
remarkable new insight altered her relationship with her father, a
practising Catholic priest.
Paperback: 978-1-78535-254-6 ebook: 978-1-78535-255-3

The Ecology of the Soul
A Manual of Peace, Power and Personal Growth for Real People
in the Real World
Aidan Walker
Balance your own inner Ecology of the Soul to regain your
natural state of peace, power and wellbeing.
Paperback: 978-1-78279-850-7 ebook: 978-1-78279-849-1

Not I, Not other than I
The Life and Teachings of Russel Williams
Steve Taylor, Russel Williams
The miraculous life and inspiring teachings of one of the World's
greatest living Sages.
Paperback: 978-1-78279-729-6 ebook: 978-1-78279-728-9

On the Other Side of Love
A woman's unconventional journey towards wisdom
Muriel Maufroy
When life has lost all meaning, what do you do?
Paperback: 978-1-78535-281-2 ebook: 978-1-78535-282-9

Practicing A Course In Miracles
A translation of the Workbook in plain language, with
mentor's notes
Elizabeth A. Cronkhite
The practical second and third volumes of The Plain-Language
A Course In Miracles.
Paperback: 978-1-84694-403-1 ebook: 978-1-78099-072-9

Quantum Bliss
The Quantum Mechanics of Happiness, Abundance, and Health
George S. Mentz
Quantum Bliss is the breakthrough summary of success and
spirituality secrets that customers have been waiting for.
Paperback: 978-1-78535-203-4 ebook: 978-1-78535-204-1

The Upside Down Mountain
Mags MacKean
A must-read for anyone weary of chasing success and happiness
– one woman's inspirational journey swapping the uphill slog for
the downhill slope.
Paperback: 978-1-78535-171-6 ebook: 978-1-78535-172-3

Your Personal Tuning Fork
The Endocrine System
Deborah Bates
Discover your body's health secret, the endocrine system, and
'twang' your way to sustainable health!
Paperback: 978-1-84694-503-8 ebook: 978-1-78099-697-4